Birds of the World

AMERICAN MUSEUM OF NATURAL HISTORY

When it opened in 1902, the Museum's **Hall of North American Birds** was the first space in the world devoted to habitat dioramas. It was created by Museum ornithologist Frank M. Chapman, whose grasp of the power of the diorama paved the way for millions of Museum visitors to lose themselves in these engaging windows into the natural world.

Known today as the **Leonard C. Sanford Hall of North American Birds**, the gallery features dioramas of several places where bird species were threatened by habitat loss or hunting. Chapman, an ardent advocate for conservation, helped shape the views of President Theodore Roosevelt, a fellow birdwatcher who established America's first federal bird reservation in 1903 in Florida. A bird sanctuary near Sagamore Hill, Roosevelt's beloved home near Oyster Bay, New York, is depicted in a diorama in the Museum's Theodore Roosevelt Memorial Hall.

A few bird species can be found worldwide, but most have adapted to a particular region—sometimes in remarkable ways. The twelve dioramas in the Museum's **Hall of Birds of the World** each depict a major biome—a region with a particular community of living things, such as desert or tropical rainforest—along with representative bird species.

The American Museum of Natural History in New York City is one of the world's preeminent scientific, educational, and cultural institutions, drawing millions of visitors each year. Visit amnh.org for more information.

AMERICAN MUSEUM ᵒᶠ NATURAL HISTORY

Pomegranate

All of the dioramas depicted in these line drawings are found at the American Museum of Natural History in New York City.

1. **Birds of the East African Plains**
   Kedong Valley, Northwest of Nairobi, Kenya
   Hall of Birds of the World

2. **Passenger Pigeons** (*Ectopistes migratorius*)
   New York, Foraging for the Acorns of the Pin Oak
   (*Quercus palustris*)
   Hall of New York City Birds

3. **Birds of Cuthbert Rookery**
   Southern Florida, Everglades National Park
   Leonard C. Sanford Hall of North American Birds

4. **Eastern Marsh Birds**
   The Marshes Bordering the Hackensack River and
   Newark Bay, New Jersey
   Leonard C. Sanford Hall of North American Birds

5. **Great Egret** (*Ardea alba*)
   South Carolina
   Leonard C. Sanford Hall of North American Birds

6. **Sandhill Crane** (*Grus canadensis*)
   Prairie and Marsh of the Florida Interior
   Leonard C. Sanford Hall of North American Birds

7. **Birds of the High Andes**
   View Near Mt. Aconcagua, Argentina
   Hall of Birds of the World

8. **Golden Eagle** (*Aquila chrysaetos*)
   Found in Europe, Asia, and North America
   Leonard C. Sanford Hall of North American Birds

9. **Birds of Australia**
   Blue Mountains of New South Wales, Australia
   Hall of Birds of the World

10. **Birds of South Georgia**
    South Georgia Island, 1,200 Miles East of Cape Horn
    Hall of Birds of the World

11. **Birds of Laysan Island**
    Hawaiian Archipelago
    Whitney Memorial Hall of Oceanic Birds

12. **Birds of New Zealand**
    Historic Depiction of Lake Brunner in the
    South Island Alps of New Zealand
    Whitney Memorial Hall of Oceanic Birds

13. **Wild Turkey** (*Meleagris gallopavo*)
    Slaty Fork, West Virginia
    Leonard C. Sanford Hall of North American Birds

14. **Boobies** (*Sula leucogaster*) **and Frigatebirds**
    (*Fregata magnificens*)
    Cay Verde, The Bahamas
    Leonard C. Sanford Hall of North American Birds

15. **Birds of the Gobi Desert**
    Tsagan Nor (White Lake), Central Asia
    Hall of Birds of the World

16. **Ostrich** (*Struthio camelus*) **and Warthog**
    (*Phacochoerus africanus*)
    Kedong Valley, 50 Miles West of Nairobi, Kenya
    Akeley Hall of African Mammals

17. **Peruvian Guano Islands**
    Bay of Pisco, Peru, From the Southern Island of the
    Chincha Group
    Whitney Memorial Hall of Oceanic Birds

18. **Birds of the East African Plains**
    Kedong Valley, Northwest of Nairobi, Kenya
    Hall of Birds of the World

19. **Birds of Cuthbert Rookery**
    Southern Florida, Everglades National Park
    Leonard C. Sanford Hall of North American Birds

Pomegranate Communications, Inc.
19018 NE Portal Way, Portland OR 97230
800 227 1428   www.pomegranate.com

Pomegranate's mission is to invigorate, illuminate, and inspire through art.

© 2017 American Museum of Natural History, New York
Photographs © AMNH. Photography by Craig Chesek, Denis Finnin,
Roderick Mickens, and Matt Shanley, AMNH.

Item No. CB185

Designed by Patrice Morris

Printed in Korea

26 25 24 23 22 21 20 19 18 17   10 9 8 7 6 5 4 3 2 1

Distributed by Pomegranate Europe Ltd.
'number three', Siskin Drive, Middlemarch Business Park
Coventry CV3 4FJ, UK
+44 (0)24 7621 4461   sales@pomegranate.com

1. Birds of the East African Plains

PIGGLE-do Birds 2. Passenger Pigeons (*Ectopistes migratorius*)

3. **Birds of Cuthbert Rookery**

4. Eastern Marsh Birds

5. Great Egret (*Ardea alba*)

6. **Sandhill Crane** (*Grus canadensis*)

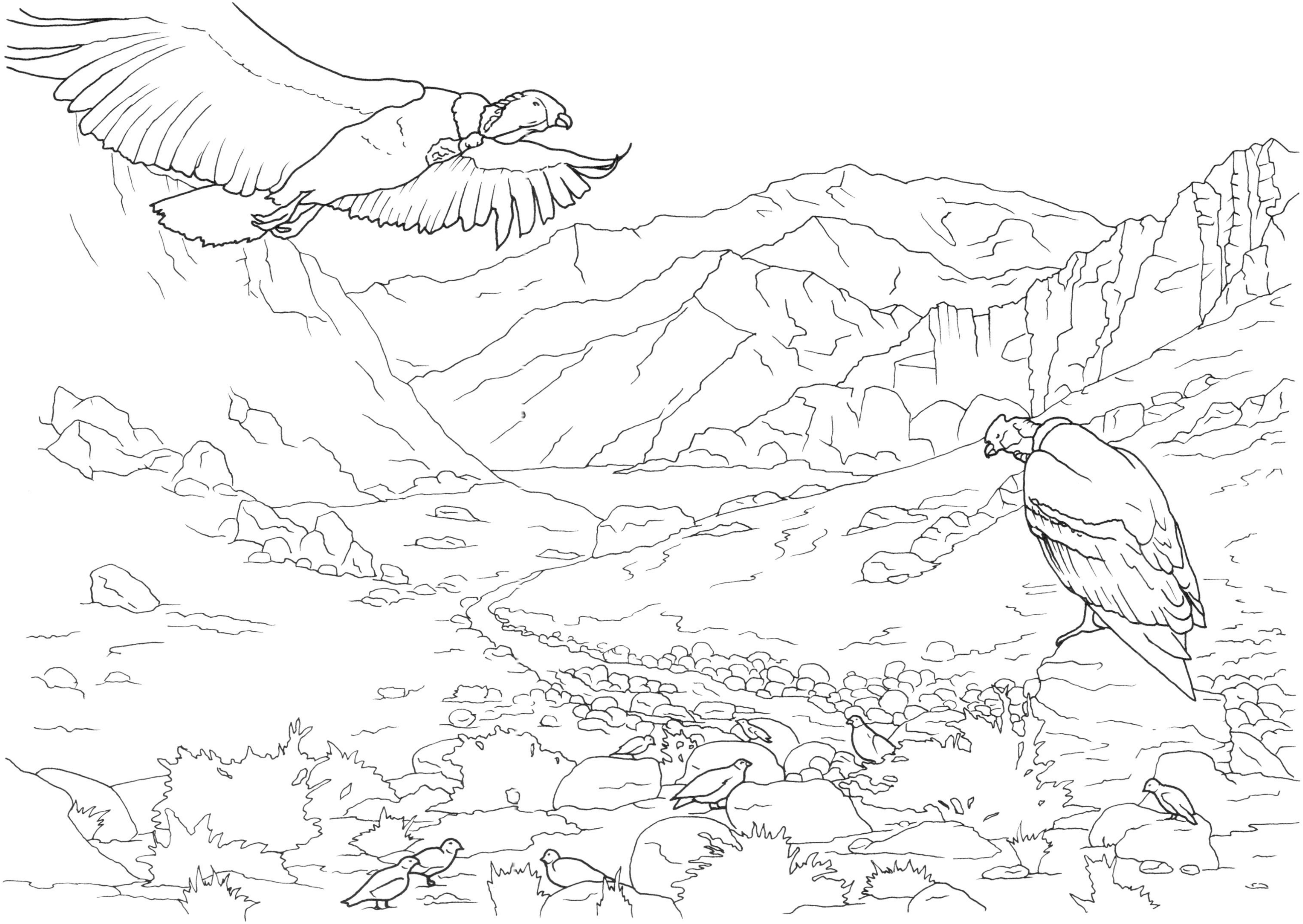

7. **Birds of the High Andes**

8. **Golden Eagle** (*Aquila chrysaetos*)

9. Birds of Australia

10. **Birds of South Georgia**

11. Birds of Laysan Island

12. **Birds of New Zealand**

13. **Wild Turkey** (*Meleagris gallopavo*)

14. **Boobies** (*Sula leucogaster*) **and Frigatebirds** (*Fregata magnificens*)

15. **Birds of the Gobi Desert**

16. **Ostrich** (*Struthio camelus*) **and Warthog** (*Phacochoerus africanus*)

17. Peruvian Guano Islands

18. **Birds of the East African Plains**

19. **Birds of Cuthbert Rookery**

Draw and color your own picture here!

Draw and color your own picture here!

Draw and color your own picture here!

Draw and color your own picture here!